To:

_____

From:

_____

Date:

_____

© Kathleen D. Mailer – Gideon's Army

101 Things That YOU ARE

Getting back to the basics of self-love

by Kathleen D. Mailer

Copyright © 2016 Kathleen D. Mailer

ISBN 978-1-897054-83-3

Published by: Aurora Publishing – a Division of: Doing Business God's Way International Inc.

101 Things That YOU ARE, Getting back to the basics of self-love by Kathleen D. Mailer

No part of this publication may be reproduced, stored in a retrieval system or transmitted in any form or by any means, electronic, mechanical, photocopying, recording or otherwise, without the written permission of the publisher.

The publisher gratefully acknowledges the many publishers and individuals who granted our *Walking in Your Destiny* stories permission to reprint in the cited material.

Connect with the Author: 587-333-5127 OR www.KathleenMailer.com

Dedication

This is the 3rd Edition of this tiny little book. I am amazed at the outpouring of women's hearts as they continue to ask me to 'revive' it. So, for you my friends....

This book is dedicated to Women everywhere who need to know that they make a difference. This is for YOU to help yourself recharge and to remember the basics from which you came.

It is for Self, Mothers, Daughters, Sisters and Friends.

****

At the time of its first printing my daughter was my pride and joy – and a young girl. As of this edition, she is now fully grown and married.

I would like to take just a quick moment to dedicate this book – to the fourth woman in my life- who has inspired me to be more, do more and love more.

Dannielle Somerville, I love you with all of my heart. This book reminds me of you. I love who we have become. We are not just mother and daughter, but true friends.

You are everything that I could have ever hoped for and so much more.

I thank God multiple times a day – and I look forward to the next stage in our life together.

May God bless you and keep you always,
Love Mom

****

This is a celebration of who and what a woman is. Who are we? We are the most incredible and complex beings that were created by God to make this world a beautiful and better place.

This book was inspired by three of my most favorite women in the world.

My Mom: she, who is no longer on this earth, but is always in my heart, I miss you terribly but am very excited that one day we will be reunited in our eternal home. All that I am, I learned from you, either directly or indirectly.

My two older sisters: I was going to call my big sisters, but I just know instinctively that once they read this passage I would be stuffed head first into the garbage can. I guess some things we never really grow out of.

My sister Pat, who is my 'ear' to the past helping me decipher how my adult life is shaped from past perceptions that I may not remember so well. Always there to lend her support and a hand when I get scared and need someone to hold on to in the dark.

My sister Sherry, who is not only my 'words' of common sense but she helps guide me in the ways of the world that I am unsure of. She can be absolutely counted on to be kind-hearted, considerate, caring and gentle. She always thinks of others first.

Together, I believe, they were sent to me by God. Truly!

Our Mom would be proud to see how they took over to help me through a stage of life when most women need their mother more than anything. This is a time when a woman becomes a 'friend' with their Mom and is schooled in the fun art of sharing all that we are.

I read a quote that I think sums up my relationship with my sisters.

"... If we believed in the media we would think the only significant relationship in our lives is a romantic one. Yet sisterhood is probably the one that will last longer than any other ... a sister will always be around." *Jane Dowdeswell.*

I pray that you, my dear reader, get what you need from this book to recharge, refuel and regain your sense of worth and your strength so that you can continue a journey full of exciting adventures.

There is more!

A special, heartfelt shout out to my book team. A Book is NEVER a Book – it is always so much more! It is a 'purpose' designed by God, to gather together his children to do something GREAT for Him and give Him the glory!

Daniela Peregrina, who translated this into Spanish for us, I thank you! Now we can share this special message with our wonderful Spanish speaking friends around the world! May God bless you as you use your gifts for the world. *Gracias!*

Ruth Yesmaniski, watching God work through you has always been such a pleasure. I don't know what I would do without you. Thank you!

To my beautiful friends and nieces, thank you for the pictures you added to the book. YOU MADE IT PERFECT. I love you with all of my heart!

How To Use This Book:

There are three specific and special ways in which this book can be used.

1. **Give a gift from the heart** to the woman/women in your life that is/are very special to you. If you give this book a quick read you can see that most everything you read directly relates to that special female that makes such an impact on you and your life. While it is sometimes difficult to express your feelings, let this book help you put into words all that you are feeling

2. **If this book was a gift** to you, please read it through as you picture the smiling face of the one that gave it to you from his/her heart.

3. **If you have bought this book for yourself**, let this be a celebration for you. Read 101 Things That YOU Are! --- remember YOU ARE those things and cherish these facts as truth.

Enjoy your journey through the pages of this book!

© Kathleen D. Mailer, Getting Ready for Greater Things

101 Things That YOU ARE!

Every day we all need to be reminded that we are important and that we matter to not only the world we live in, but to those closest to us. Unfortunately too many times we forget to give ourselves the same courtesy and treatment we give others.

After all, our job is to influence others, help them be all they are meant to be, equip them with their emotional needs, give guidance to our family, special people in our life, friends and others we come into contact with.

- We are to juggle multiple schedules, create a loving environment and become all we are meant to be.

- We are to educate ourselves and others in so many specialized areas. As a result we tend to read from, listen to, and chat with mentors who help to make this transition a bit easier –but it never seems to be enough.

- We wear many hats, it is true, but we tend to 'lose' the hat that says "love thyself!"

So I take this time to acknowledge YOU. You who always does for others without asking for anything in return. I have this to say.

YOU ARE!

1. First and foremost a child of God. He who is the Most High. He who created everything beautiful, including you.

2. Astonishing and incredible, beyond mere words. What you can do in such a relatively short period of time is pure amazement.

3. Powerful . How? You are an influencer and a friend. How you quiet my heart when I hurt.

4. Intoxicating. Your energy calms and soothes, excites and thrills even the most dull and dreary of us.

5. A Graduate of the Common-Sense School. Making things clear when taking the time to think of what to do; 95% of the time you can figure it out.

6. A friend. The deep Grand Canyon type of friendship that will never falter or fade.

© Kathleen D. Mailer, Don't Look Back

7. Compassionate. Saving the pity for a victim, but understanding for me.

8. Munificent. Always giving everything you have, everything you are and everything you could possibly be.

9. Tough. Only when I need to know that sometimes I don't understand the full truth of how life is, but you do. You stick to your guns to help me when I can't see the full picture.

10.   A Rock. One who is my foundation in this fragile world we call home. Steady and unfailing

11. Independent, yet Interdependent. You can stand on your own two feet but you choose to walk with me and stand beside me letting us hold each other up as we go.

© Kathleen D. Mailer, Position To Prosper

12. A mirror. Shining back to me the things I love about myself and sometimes, the things I don't like so much.

13. A great listener. You know just when to listen and when to give me advice.

14. A comedienne. Laughing and making jokes at the perfect time. Always bringing me out of my funk and helping me see the lighter side of life.

15. An encourager. Always cheering me on to follow my dreams and not to just become, but envelope the essence of who I truly am.

16. A mentor. Paving the way for me by taking life's blows, softening them and warning me they are coming.

17. My Protector. Not only do you shield me from shattering pieces of glass that explode when the windshield of life is hit with a force stronger than a tornado wind, but you also stand by my side telling those with little good to say that they know nothing about who I really am.

18. My personal historian. One who shares my past, present and future.

19. An Accountability Coach. Keeping me accountable and reminding me that my word is everything.

20. A doctor. Healing everything from a cut or bruise to a broken heart.

21. My home. A place where I am sheltered by the storms... A comfortable stress-free place to call my own.

22.	My Acceptance. Emanating unconditional love from your heart to mine.

23.	My lighthouse. You guide me through the fog and in the darkness of night.

24.	My teammate. Working together to uncover life's special gifts every day and then deliciously discussing the blessings that are tied to each and every one.

25.   My world. I understand now, because of you, that we not only live in this world but we have the world live in us.

26.   My vacation. Giving me a four day retreat when I get to spend quality time with you.

© Kathleen D. Mailer, Peace in the Night

27.   Someone not to grow old with, but rather ripen with; like the finest fruit on the strongest of trees.

28.   Like my diary. You are my sounding board and a keeper of all of my deep dark secrets.

29.   My happiest moments in life. Memories that last forever and warm my heart.

30.   My Advisor. Again, not only knowing when to give advice but you are also smart enough to be unattached to the outcome of my choice to take the advice or not.

© Kathleen D. Mailer, Serenity

31.   My lucky charm. I consider myself not only blessed but the luckiest person on earth that you are in my life.

32. Better than Santa Claus. Knowing if I have been bad or good, and not really caring.

33. My Competition. If I believed in it. You give me just enough to measure against someone like you so that I can strive to become a better person.

34. My Gift. A present from God himself. You are in my life for better, and for worse. I choose to keep you next to my heart.

35.   My Consoler. Not trying to erase the painful hurts of what is to be a life experience, but helping me understand something that doesn't make sense.

36.   My chrysalis. Holding me tight in a cocoon of love and then when I am ready for change you encourage me to do it flamboyantly, immediately and wholeheartedly.

37.   My living space. Letting me live and let live. Seeing both my boring and tedious side as well as the effervescent piece of me and being ok with both those things.

38. My shield. Together, because we know each other so well, we are a force to reckon with so watch out world!

© Kathleen D. Mailer, She Fights!

39. My song. Sure we have differences and we don't always have the same opinions but I couldn't live without our song.

40. My tribe, my clanswoman. Throughout life's triumphs and catastrophes we could not live without our clan.

41. My expression. No language is ever so sweet as the knowing you understand my expressions and what they truly mean. You know my snarls, my looks of shocked surprise

and skepticism as well as sniffs, gasps and sighs.

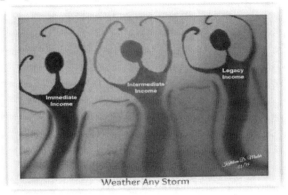

© Kathleen D. Mailer, Weather Any Storm

42. My legacy. Through you and your ways of sharing who I am my life will live on long after you and I are gone.

43. My kindred spirit. Sometimes we really stretch the chain of the bond we have, but we will never break it.

44.   My gardener. Planting seeds of inspiration and motivation deep within my soul.

© Kathleen D. Mailer, God is Fighting For You.

45.   My earth. Giving me a place to grow and nourishment to thrive.

46.   My rain. Drenching the seeds of thrills and excitement growing inside of me.

© Kathleen D. Mailer, Times of Refreshing

47.   My sunshine. Pouring out the heat and warmth and giving me a place to aspire to.

48.   My web in life. An intricate meshing of heart and soul and energy to make sure my dreams stick like glue.

49.   My reinforcement. Reminding me that I must do it by myself but I never have to do it alone.

50.   My Winter. Hot chocolate and an open fire.

51.   My Summer.   Sandy white beaches and golden sunshine.

© Kathleen D. Mailer, The Beach

52.   My Fall. Fiery oranges, ruby reds, deep lush greens with a splash of golden yellows.

53.   My Spring.   Intoxicating perfume on the wings of a fresh breeze.

54. My abstract artist. Painting my life with interesting parallels.

55. My right hand. Helping out whenever the need arises.

56. My tight rope walker. Keeping me moving forward while I balance high above the 'neigh sayers' below.

© Kathleen D. Mailer, The Last Day of the Old Me, SUNDOWN

57. My race car. Navigating me through the road rage in life and helping me get to where I need to go in record-breaking time.

© Kathleen D. Mailer, My Lord

58. My map. Giving me directions when the construction ahead signs show up in my life; showing me that there are many ways to reach my goal, not just one, lonely, solitary road.

59.   My solace. When I must seek peace and quiet.

© Kathleen D. Mailer, Peace At Dawn

60.   My priceless heirloom. Your character and ways I will treasure always and pass on to my family for generations to come.

61. My hero. Someone I can look up to. I know you will give me a hand up and not a hand out.

62. My partner in crime. Sharing my mischievous moments in life, making it easier to get away with almost anything.

63. My bubble bath. Soothing, nurturing, calming.

64. My telephone. Knowing you are just a phone call away.

65. My treadmill. Going, going, going- stopping just long enough to let me on or off.

66. My mountain. Strong, steady and unwavering.

67. My tree. Protecting, growing and deeply rooted.

68. My waterfall. Effervescent, refreshing, renewing

69.   My lush green grass. Soft, squishy, cool as I run bare foot across the lawn.

70.   Private Jokester. Remembering the feuds and the fun and laughing behind everyone's back.

71.   An angel. My own personal someone to watch over me.

72.   My rainbow. Coloring my world.

73. My pot of gold. Priceless.

74. My humanitarian. Reminding me that a whole world is out there that needs me as much as I need them.

© Kathleen D. Mailer, All That I am

75. My truth. You remind me that one is not born a woman, one becomes one. I see this is true in you.

76. My doorway. When one door closes, you help me find a new one and push me through!

© Kathleen D. Mailer, Choices

77. My dress rehearsal for life. I get a trial run before I 'show off' to the rest of the world.

78. My private dancer. Graceful, elegant, and eloquent.

79. My provider. Providing me with things too numerous, that I cannot mention them all.

80. My manners. What simple thing is 'please' and 'thank you'? 'tis you in a nutshell.

81. My circle of love. No beginning. No end.

82. My dog. (NO! I am NOT calling you names!) You are a loyal companion.

83.   Just (justice) - but as I mentioned earlier, nonjudgmental.

84.   Beautiful. Beyond words.

85. Integrity. In every sense of the word.

86. A timeless truth.

87. Someone who can transcend age, gaining only wisdom.

88. The essence of inner peace.

89.   The brink of excitement and joy.

90.   The cat's meow.

91.   The spark that ignites fireworks and starts the show-stopping gasp in the crowd.

92.   The 'oooh, awe' the is elicited from a crowd of amazed and mesmerized individuals.

© Kathleen D. Mailer, A Fork In The Road

93.   The whipped cream on top of my hot chocolate.

94.   A breath of fresh air I inhale after it has just rained and I am on my walk in the woods.

95.   A combination of a rainbow and the pot of gold.

96.   A fluffy, white, puff of a cloud worthy of my intense gaze as it floats across the sky.

97.   A finely-tuned engine roaring with precision and perfect timing.

98.   A rose that lasts forever, rich in both fragrance and color.

99. A tulip that brings hope, for all to see that it is spring.

100. The bounce in my step.

101. The sound of incredible bubbling laughter that erupts from an 8-month old baby's belly; infectious, exceptional and out of this world.

And... one extra just because.....
102. A million holidays – birthdays, New Year's, Christmas, Easter, St. Patrick's Day, Thanksgiving – all rolled into one.

With all my heart, with all my soul, I pray you understand who you REALLY are.
I pray you know how you impact others.
I pray you get the message of how special you truly are.

I pray you treat yourself with the love you deserve.

May your life be filled with the very essence of your being.

About The Author:

Kathleen D. Mailer is affectionately known around the world as the "International Business Evangelist". As a #1 Best Selling Author of over 46 books, she is dedicated and determined to HELP CHRISTIANS become SUCCESSFUL PUBLISHED AUTHORS.

In her words, *"You better believe there is POWER in your TESTIMONY!"*

She accomplishes this through both her world-famous Boot Camp,

"A Book Is Never A Book"
(www.ABookIsNeverABook.com) and through her new on-line mentorship programs coming soon to:
www.ChristianAuthorsGetPaid.com.

She is also Publisher of the International Magazine - *Today's Businesswoman Magazine* (#1 Resource for Christian Women in Business); which brings quality, affordable mentorship for the businesswoman who is looking to achieve entrepreneurial success, God's way.

Kathleen passionately believes that her business is her ministry. **That contagious fire is evident on every platform she speaks.** It doesn't matter if it's on a stage in the business world; from a pulpit in front of a church; pouring out in leadership conferences; or sitting in your living room - **taking care of God's 'Family Business' is her TOP priority.** With this in mind, she and her husband Dan have made it their mission to eradicate poverty in the nations, one business person at a time.

To invite Kathleen to speak to your: group, organization, church, or for your event:
t: @KathleenMailer,
fb: KathleenDMailer -PUBLIC FIGURE,
li: Kathleen Mailer
w: www.KathleenMailer.com,
em: getbooked@shaw.ca

Partial list of her best-selling books: *Prepare To Prosper, Taking Your Business To A Higher Level*; *Walking In Your Destiny, Moving Through The Fear;,* and COMING SOON, *Walking in the Wake of the Holy Spirit- Living An Ordinary Life With An Extraordinary God!*

"God gives us a business so we can DO God's Business!" – Kathleen D. Mailer

Walking In Your Destiny,
Moving Through the Fear

Deep inside, your heart yearns to walk boldly through obstacles and storms in life, marching for-ward 'on fire' for the Lord.

Every time you decide that "to-day is the day" to do that, you find yourself paralyzed with fear. Don't STAY stuck!

Inside the pages of this powerful and anointed book, Godly wo-men share their hearts, struggles and strategies.

Find the support, encouragement and next level thinking you need in order help you move past the fear and embrace the fullness of your destiny.

ORDER TODAY --- www.Amazon.com

Walking In Your Destiny,
Living in HIS Increase

INCREASE IN THE NAME OF JESUS!

Is there anything better? Inside these pages you will find real life stories of incredible women who, despite their circumstances, found their life filled with His Increase: increased finances, increased health, increased favour, increased grace, increased relationships, increased influence, increased wisdom, and so much more!

We pray that the God of Angel Armies would minister to you through these incredible stories – and you would find a renewing of HOPE, an INCREASE of FAITH, and the COURAGE to take action in your own life.

This book will be a favorite among **women's bible studies** (taking a different chapter each month – applying the wisdom and praying for one another) or at a **weekly 'Doing Business God's Way' business meeting,** and a **great addition to every guest's conference ticket** to help position them to receive.

ARE YOU READY?

ORDER TODAY
www.Amazon.com

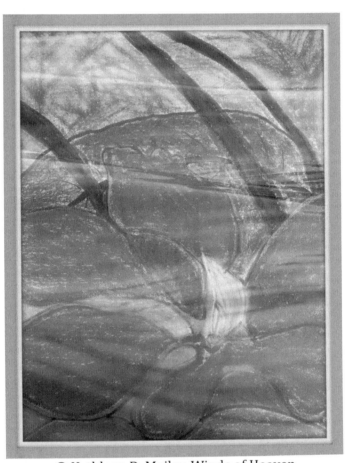

© Kathleen D. Mailer, Winds of Heaven

Made in the USA
Charleston, SC
10 June 2016